WALKIN[G] TO WISDOM

LITERATURE GUIDE SERIES

The Lion, the Witch and the Wardrobe

C.S. Lewis

by Kelly Warner

Inklings Collection

Walking to Wisdom Literature Guide: The Lion, the Witch and the Wardrobe

Version 1.0
ISBN: 978-1-60051-244-5

Classical Academic Press
2151 Market Street
Camp Hill, PA 17011

www.ClassicalAcademicPress.com

Series Editor: Christine Perrin
Editor: Janet Dixon
Cover Design: Kristin Roach
Interior Design: Lenora Riley & Kristin Roach
Illustrations: Gretchen Nesbit

PGP.09.14

Walking to Wisdom Literature Guide: *The Lion, the Witch and the Wardrobe*

Table of Contents

Introduction to Students

Dear Students,

We are excited that you have the privilege of reading *The Lion, the Witch and the Wardrobe* alongside a mentor (the writer of this guide) who will lead you "further up and further in" (C.S. Lewis's words in *The Last Battle*). We aim to give you a delightful experience with this book and, in the process, to share practices that we have learned that will help you become a good reader:

- reading carefully
- taking time to absorb a book
- paying attention to details as well as to great ideas over the whole book
- learning to mark up a book
- taking a few notes while reading
- learning to ask and answer good questions
- synthesizing those questions together in a piece of writing or an engaging project

If you spend a year doing all of the Inklings courses, you will not only collect some of the most important books and thoughts, but you will also have increased your abilities and pleasures as a reader.

C.S. Lewis, J.R.R. Tolkien, and Dorothy Sayers (three members of the Inklings whose work you will study in the Walking to Wisdom Literature Guides: The Inklings Collection) wrote nonfiction as well as fiction, and we begin your reading of fiction with a few select nonfiction essays they wrote on topics that overlap with the topics in the book you are reading. Part of their remarkable legacy is that they wrote about many of the same great ideas in stories, plays, and poems and in nonfiction essays. This means that reading the ideas without the stories in these nonfiction works, or "context essays," will be a significant help to you in understanding them and in fully exploring the characters, plot, and imagery. American writer Flannery O'Connor said, "Our response to life is different if we have been taught only a definition of faith than if we have trembled with Abraham as he held a knife over Isaac." This is what stories do—they give us an experience of certain knowledge, which is why how we feel about the book is part of what the book is teaching us. We have kept these things in heart and mind while making this guide for you.

We have suggested two reading schedules—one that allows ten days to study the book and the other that allows twenty. Feel free to double that to add extra time for writing and enrichment activities (found at the end of the book). Your teacher will know what is best for your schedule. We have provided you with some space for answering questions, but we recommend that you also keep your thoughts, notes, and musings in a three-ring binder (or on the computer). For the "life questions," you may want to keep a separate journal for meditative contemplation. We would like you to have as much room as you need, because you will find that the Inklings writers require a lot of space! It is highly recommended that you look up unfamiliar words found in C.S. Lewis's *The Lion, the Witch and the Wardrobe*, and keep a journal of these new vocabulary words and definitions as you work through the book and the guide.

You have the option of studying one guide or a few, or taking a year to study them all to fulfill your British literature requirement for high school English. Enjoy the study!

Scope and Sequence for the Walking to Wisdom Literature Guides: The Inklings Collection

C.S. Lewis

Context Essays (selections from these are read at the beginning of each guide): excerpts from *Mere Christianity*,[1] *The Weight of Glory*,[2] *On Stories: And Other Essays on Literature*,[3] and "Theology in Stories" by Gilbert Meilaender[4]

- *The Lion, the Witch and the Wardrobe*[5]
- *The Last Battle*[6]
- *The Screwtape Letters*[7]
- *Till We Have Faces*[8]

Dorothy Sayers

Context Essays: excerpts from *Letters to a Diminished Church*[9]

The Man Born to Be King (twelve-play cycle integrating the four gospels)[10]

J.R.R. Tolkien

- *The Fellowship of the Ring*[11]
- *The Two Towers*[12]
- *The Return of the King*[13]

1. The Walking to Wisdom Literature Guides: The Inklings Collection is keyed to the following editions listed in these footnotes: C.S. Lewis, *Mere Christianity* (New York: HarperOne, 2009).
2. C.S. Lewis, *The Weight of Glory* (New York: HarperOne, 2009).
3. C.S. Lewis, *On Stories: And Other Essays on Literature* (San Diego: Harcourt Books, 1966).
4. Gilbert Meilaender, "Theology in Stories: C.S. Lewis and the Narrative Quality of Experience," *Word and World* 1/3 (1981): 222, http://wordandworld.luthersem.edu/content/pdfs/1-3_Experience/1-3_Meilaender.pdf.
5. C.S. Lewis, *The Chronicles of Narnia* (New York: HarperCollins, 2001).
6. Lewis, *Chronicles.*
7. C.S. Lewis, *The Screwtape Letters* (New York: HarperOne, 2009).
8. C.S. Lewis, *Till We Have Faces* (Orlando, FL: Harcourt, Brace, & Co., 1980).
9. Dorothy Sayers, *Letters to a Dimished Church* (Nashville, TN: Thomas Nelson, 2004).
10. Dorothy Sayers, *The Man Born to Be King: A Play-Cycle on the Life of Our Lord and Saviour, Jesus Christ, Written for Broadcasting* (Grand Rapids, MI: Eerdmans, 1943). Reprinted with permission by Classical Academic Press, 2014.
11. J.R.R. Tolkien, *The Fellowship of the Ring* (Boston: Mariner Books, 2005).
12. J.R.R. Tolkien, *The Two Towers* (Boston: Mariner Books, 2005).
13. J.R.R. Tolkien, *The Return of the King* (Boston: Mariner Books, 2005).

The Inklings

The Inklings was an informal literary discussion group associated with the University of Oxford, England, for nearly two decades between the early 1930s and late 1949.[1] The Inklings were writers, including C.S. Lewis, J.R.R. Tolkien, Dorothy Sayers, and Charles Williams, who shared a love of similar stories and a remarkable commitment to ideas they shared. Their literary philosophies tended to depart from the period in which they were writing (modernist, 1900–1950) as did their cultural values. They liked to walk together and meet regularly to read their work aloud to one another

"Properly speaking," wrote Warren Lewis (brother of C.S.), "the Inklings was neither a club nor a literary society, though it partook of the nature of both. There were no rules, officers, agendas, or formal elections."[2] While Dorothy Sayers did not attend the meetings herself, partly because she didn't live in the same town or teach at Oxford, she is often claimed as an Inkling, as a friend of Lewis and Charles Williams. Her correspondence with both was avid and their work concerned with many of the same subjects, characters, and plots. They were a great encouragement to one other. Lewis even read Sayers's play cycle, *The Man Born to Be King* (which is included in our literature guide series), each year during the Lenten period.

Readings and discussions of the members' unfinished works were the principal purposes of meetings. Tolkien's *The Lord of the Rings*, Lewis's *Out of the Silent Planet*, and Williams's *All Hallows' Eve* were among the first novels the Inklings read to one another. Tolkien's fictional Notion Club (see *Sauron Defeated*) was based on the Inklings. Meetings were not all serious; the Inklings amused themselves by having competitions to see who could read notoriously bad prose for the longest without laughing.[3]

Until late 1949, Inklings readings and discussions usually occurred during Thursday evenings in C.S. Lewis's college rooms at Magdalen College. The Inklings and friends were also known to gather informally on Tuesdays at midday at a local public house, The Eagle and Child.

We hope that you will keep the spirit of the Inklings alive in your own study of this guide by working out your own responses to their work in community and conversation as well as laboring over your writing and sharing it with fellow travelers seeking to walk a similar path. Consider studying this course online at Scholé Academy (classicalacademicpress.com/online-courses/).

1. Clyde S. Kilby and Marjorie Lamp Mead, eds., *Brothers and Friends: The Diaries of Major Warren Hamilton Lewis* (San Francisco: Harper & Row, 1982), 230.
2. Bruce L. Edwards, *Apologist, Philosopher, and Theologian*, vol. 3 of *C.S. Lewis: Life, Works, and Legacy* (Westport, CT: Praegar, 2007), 279.
3. "War of Words over World's Worst Writer," *Culture Northern Ireland*, May 9, 2008, <http://www.culturenorthernireland.org/article/1739/war-of-words-over-world-s-worst-writer?search=inklings&rpg=1>.

Daily Reading Outlines for C.S. Lewis's *The Lion, the Witch and the Wardrobe*

Schedule 1

This schedule requires you to read two to three chapters per day of *The Lion, the Witch and the Wardrobe* for six days, in addition to the context essays.

Day 1: Context essay excerpt from *The Weight of Glory*: "On Forgiveness"

Day 2: Context essay excerpts from *Mere Christianity*: "The Great Sin" and "Charity"

Day 3: Context essay excerpt from *The Weight of Glory*: "The Weight of Glory"

Day 4: Context essay "Theology in Stories" by Gilbert Meilaender[1] for grades 10 through 12 ***or*** context essay from *On Stories*: "Sometimes Fairy Stories May Say Best What's to Be Said" for grades 7 through 9

Day 5: Chapters 1–3

Day 6: Chapters 4–6

Day 7: Chapters 7–9

Day 8: Chapters 10–12

Day 9: Chapters 13–15

Day 10: Chapters 16–17

Your teacher will take as many extra days as needed to work on essay and enrichment activities.

Schedule 2

This schedule will double your time on each assignment and take two days for each unit to make a twenty-day program. Your teacher may choose to add another week for the final writing assignment.

Days 1–2: Context essay excerpt from *Mere Christianity*: "On Forgiveness"

Days 3–4: Context essay excerpts from *Mere Christianity*: "The Great Sin" and "Charity"

Days 5–6: Context essay excerpt from *The Weight of Glory*: "The Weight of Glory"

Days 7–8: Context essay, "Theology in Stories" by Gilbert Meilaender[2] for grades 10 through 12 ***or*** context essay from *On Stories*: "Sometimes Fairy Stories May Say Best What's to Be Said" for grades 7 through 9

Days 9–10: Chapters 1–3

Days 11–12: Chapters 4–6

Days 13–14: Chapters 7–9

Days 15–16: Chapters 10–12

Days 17–18: Chapters 13–15

Days 19–20: Chapters 16–17

Your teacher will take as many extra days as needed to work on essay and enrichment activities.

1. This essay can be found at <http://wordandworld.luthersem.edu/content/pdfs/1-3_Experience/1-3_Meilaender.pdf>.
2. This essay can be found at <http://wordandworld.luthersem.edu/content/pdfs/1-3_Experience/1-3_Meilaender.pdf>.

Elements in the Literature Guide

Make Notes: Possess the Book

Becoming a reader is all about learning to pay attention and gather the details to relish and realize the significance and unity of what you are reading. Try using the following symbols or making up your own system that covers the same basics. Underline interesting passages. Write in the margins so that you can go back to reference what you wrote to make your Great Ideas Quotes pages, answer questions, hold discussions, and support points you make in your writing assignments. Here is a simple marking system that we have found effective:

- * This is important or delightful.
- ? I have a question.
- ?? I'm confused.
- ! This is surprising or exciting to me.
- **T** This could relate to one of the themes or motifs of the book.
- ✓ This relates to something else I have read.
- **X** This is part of the conflict or the problem of the story.
- **C** This is significant in defining this character.

Tracing the Great Ideas

As you read, choose quotes related to the following great ideas topics (or themes) so that you can trace them all the way through the book. (Please remember that you are welcome to find your own great ideas themes in addition to ours.) Then be on the lookout for how they are worked out in each particular context. Some chapters may contain quotes relating to only one great ideas topic, or may contain several topics. Write the quotes on the Great Ideas Quotes pages. (See page 8 for an example of how to record the quotations.) At the end of the guide you will reflect upon the themes of the course and choose one from which you will develop an argumentative essay. You may use our great idea definition for your essay's thesis or create a thesis of your own.

Great Ideas

Myth, rhymes, legends as knowledge: Lewis believes the real purpose of myth, rhyme and legend is to communicate truth. Understanding the purpose of myth also helped Lewis accept Christianity.

Virtue and moral choice: Virtue isn't an innate quality, but something that develops every day when we make decisions. Each decision builds momentum; it's easier to continue choosing virtue if you have already made a good decision. However, anyone can choose to do the right thing. In *The Lion, the Witch and the Wardrobe,* virtue is shown by a character's choice to love another person, or by his choice to seek forgiveness.

Education/The testing or ordeal: Traditional education models failed Lewis, and he remains unsurprisingly critical of those schools in *The Lion, the Witch and the Wardrobe* which don't teach logic or engage the imagination. As an alternative method of education, Lewis suggests learning occurs through experiences and ordeals.

Evil and vice: In *The Lion, the Witch and the Wardrobe* we see the characteristics of vice mainly through two characters: the White Witch and Edmund. From their stories, we can see that evil is a deceptive, lesser substitute for good, and ultimately destructive force.

Landscape: The dynamic changes of the land parallel the dramatic shift of power from the queen to Aslan. Lewis uses the metaphors and winter and spring to illustrate the spiritual change sweeping over Narnia with Aslan's return. The landscape imagery is powerful, because we have personal experience with both winter and spring.

***Responding to Aslan/*Sehnsucht:** Characters' responses to Aslan—or even just the name of Aslan—reveal their spiritual state. Additionally, every character's response is unique, highlighting Lewis belief that the relationship to God is highly personal. Our longing for Aslan is part of our relationship to Aslan.

Multiple worlds: *The Lion, the Witch and the Wardrobe* spans two worlds—ours and Narnia. The children are sent to the professor's house during London bombing raids of WWII, while Narnia is under the oppressive rule of the White Witch. What is the relationship between these two worlds? How does the narrator help us bridge these worlds? What are some images or symbols in Narnia that parallel things in our world? Look also for the references to history—such as the totalitarian state, the secret police, the bombing in London.

Deep magic: The deep magic was a set of laws placed into Narnia by the Emperor-beyond-the-Sea at the time of its creation. It was written on the stone table, the firestones on the Secret Hill, and the scepter of the Emperor-beyond-the-Sea. This law states that the White Witch is entitled to kill every traitor, and if someone denies her this right, then all of Narnia would be overturned and perish in fire and water. However, unknown to the queen, a deeper magic from before the dawn of time existed, which said that if a willing victim who had committed no treachery was killed in a traitor's stead, the stone gable would crack, and death would start working backwards. This term refers to the spiritual reality of Aslan's work in Narnia.

Forgiveness: Lewis discusses the importance of forgiveness—a forgiveness that is quite different from an excuse, a forgiveness that is costly. In Narnia, Lewis dramatically illustrates forgiveness through Edmund.

Tell It Back

This is a summary exercise, a method of narrating the chapters orally, or "telling it back." It is a wonderful option that allows you to narrate the content of each unit by oral summary—with or without a partner(s). Others have acted it out with props or sock puppets. This is a basic element of learning to read which never loses its delight and capacity to delight others. It also helps to develop a strong mental outlining ability and memory.

(Optional) We like it when people make their own illustrations for a book to enter more fully into the lives of the characters. Feel free to do so as you make your way through the book, as a chapter unit summary exercise, or afterward, when you have finished. How you feel about the book and what you are able to imagine about the book is part of what it is teaching you. Tolkien made drawings for many of his own characters.

Reading Questions

Reading questions encourage close reading of the text by asking comprehension questions. All answers are found in the text.

Discussion Questions

Discussion questions require you to synthesize the main ideas of the text that may be either explicitly or implicitly stated. Your answers to these should explain Lewis's perspective, not your own. Depending on your level, learning needs, or preference, the in-depth discussion questions may be written as short answers (one to two paragraphs), discussed with the teacher/fellow students, or simply read to inspire critical thinking.

Life Questions—Journaling Assignment

It's difficult to read any of C.S. Lewis's writing without thinking about applying his ideas to your own life. *The Lion, the Witch and the Wardrobe* is no exception. After each reading section, several "life questions" help you reflect on your own personal experiences and examine your own life in light of ideas from *The Lion, the Witch and the Wardrobe.* You may write informal responses to the life questions in a separate journal.

Write Your Own Discussion Questions

At the end of each section, create two discussion questions that you think would make for good discussion among classmates, friends, and family. These should not chiefly be questions that have a sentence-long answer, but rather questions that would stimulate a longer exchange of ideas. Use our discussion questions and life questions as guides for writing yours.

INTRODUCTION TO *THE LION, THE WITCH AND THE WARDROBE*

Lewis wrote The Chronicles of Narnia quickly—the first five in less than three years. The whole process lasted from 1948 to 1954. He wrote them at a difficult time in his life when he was caring for the mother of a close friend, Paddy Moore, whom he had met on the battlefield. Before Paddy died they promised each other to care for the other's family should they die in the war. C.S. Lewis and Mrs. Moore had a complicated relationship; at this point in time it was challenging for him to care for her. He wrote to a friend during this time, "I feel my zeal for writing, and whatever talent I originally possessed, to be decreasing; nor (I believe) do I please my readers as I used to."[1] It goes to show that we are not always the best judges of ourselves, because the coming decade was to be a fruitful one for Lewis. It was during this time he wrote The Chronicles of Narnia, *Mere Christianity, The Oxford History of English Literature*, and *Surprised by Joy*. Most of us would be happy to have written just one of these books in our lifetime.

Many people point to the morals and the allegory as the starting point for *The Lion, the Witch and the Wardrobe*, but Lewis insisted that it all began with a picture of a faun carrying an umbrella and parcels in a snowy wood, and that he'd carried that picture since he was sixteen years old. The presence of evacuated children from London during the air raids in September 1939 in his home must have helped to stir his imagination. Some of his influences in children's literature included E. Nesbit and George MacDonald. He also loved Beatrix Potter. But, of course, he'd read most of the great classics of western literature at this point and was a professor of English Language and Literature at Oxford.

There are many books that function as sources for *The Lion, the Witch and the Wardrobe*, which is a good example of how the creation process works for most writers. We are always standing on the shoulders of giants—borrowing plots and words and characters and making them our own. The pale, cruel queen, the White Witch, has precedents in Hans Christian Andersen's *Snow Queen* as well as the sorceress Circe in Homer's *Odyssey*, according to Lewis. But he also believed in the idea of archetype. An archetype is a figure that dwells in everyone's unconscious—all readers who share a similar culture also share universal images and meanings that come out in stories and dreams. This idea was first articulated by psychologist Carl Jung.

In the lion, Aslan, Lewis intended to combine the paradoxical nature of a good but fear-inducing God that inspires awe in the presence of others. In a wonderful essay from his book *On Stories* titled "Sometimes Fairy Stories May Say Best What's to Be Said" (we have the option to study this essay in this guide as well), Lewis explained his idea that fantasy would re-present the gospel in all its glory and inspire love in the readers as opposed to simple obligation. The imagination, he believed, is powerful and essential to faith. That said, however, he didn't intend these to be simply allegories for the Bible. He stated it bluntly once, saying,

> You are mistaken when you think that everything in the books "represents" something in this world. . . . I did not say to myself "Let us represent Jesus as He really is in our world by a Lion in Narnia": I said "Let us *suppose* that there were a land like Narnia and that the Son of God, as He became a Man in our world, became a Lion there, and then imagine what would happen."[2]

Lewis believed in educating the moral imagination, in moral education. He believed that the world we live in and the people we are have a nature, a way in which things objectively are—that certain attitudes are true and certain are false. In this way of thinking, moral laws are as universal and fundamental to our existence as physical laws. Teaching children to conform to what is true—such as taking up one's duties and turning away from impulses that are harmful—is the right aim of education and adults. Lewis believed there is a consensus among most religious traditions on many issues and he considered moral relativism to be dishonest. He spoke of this more explicitly in *Mere Christianity*, a book from which we use excerpts in these literature guides to help

1. David Downing, *Into the Wardrobe* (San Francisco: Jossey-Bass, 2005), 27. This is a book worthy of reading in conjunction with the literature guides.
2. Downing, 64-65.

us study the fiction. In particular, he was interested in moral choices, and we see that again and again in the world of Narnia, to which we are fully introduced in *The Lion, the Witch and the Wardrobe*, and in the lives of Peter, Susan, Edmund, and Lucy—children who become kings and queens in the course of this book.

For Further Biographical Study

Please see the following resource: http://www.cslewis.org/resource/chronocsl/. This website—created by the C.S. Lewis Foundation—suggests and links to a number of excellent sources.

Tracing the Great Ideas

You may record your Great Ideas Quotes on the pages that follow or you may want to consider placing copies of the Great Ideas Quotes pages in a three-ring notebook at the beginning of your guide work to keep a "map" of your reading.

You should feel free to shorthand quotes by listing the quote's beginning and end, then its page number, on the proper Great Ideas Quotes page.

Examples:

Great Ideas Quotes throughout the book for the theme *Myth, rhymes, legends as knowledge*

" 'A door. A door from the world of men! I have heard of such things. This may wreck all.' " (124)

shorthand version:

" 'A door. . . . I have heard of such things.' " (124)

Great Ideas Quotes throughout the Book for the Theme *Myth, rhymes, legends as knowledge*

GREAT IDEAS QUOTES THROUGHOUT THE BOOK FOR THE THEME *VIRTUE AND MORAL CHOICE*

Great Ideas Quotes throughout the Book for the Theme

Education/The testing or ordeal

Great Ideas Quotes throughout the Book for the Theme *Evil and Vice*

Great Ideas Quotes throughout the Book for the Theme *Landscape*

Great Ideas Quotes throughout the Book for the Theme *Responding to Aslan*/Sehnsucht

Great Ideas Quotes throughout the Book for the Theme *Multiple worlds*

Great Ideas Quotes throughout the Book for the Theme *Deep Magic*

Great Ideas Quotes throughout the Book for the Theme *Forgiveness*

Summarize the Context Essays

Before you start reading *The Lion, the Witch and the Wardrobe*, you will read and summarize the excerpts we have selected from *Mere Christianity*, *The Weight of Glory*, and *On Stories* books, as well as the Gilbert Meilaender essay. Then cross-check your summaries with ours (in the teacher's edition) to make sure you have covered the topic adequately. Our summaries range from 45–225 words, with the exception of "The Weight of Glory," which is longer (400 words). Your teacher will assign a word count for yours. These "context essays" will help you to understand and gain insight into many of the ideas that arise in *The Lion, the Witch and the Wardrobe*. An important part of becoming a good reader involves being able to summarize your reading in such a way that someone else can understand what you have read. Please note: if you would like to spend extra time in discussion about the essays, there is an appendix at the back of this guide with questions related to them. Otherwise, a summary will do.

"On Forgiveness" Summary (from *The Weight of Glory*, Essay 8)

"The Great Sin" Summary (from *Mere Christianity*, Book III, Chapter 8)

"Charity" Summary (from *Mere Christianity*, Book 3, Chapter 9)

"The Weight of Glory" Summary (from *The Weight of Glory*, Essay 1)

"Theology in Stories" Summary (Online Essay by Gilbert Meilaender)

"Sometimes Fairy Stories May Say Best What's to Be Said" Summary (from *On Stories*, Essay 5)

Unit 1: Chapters 1–3

Make Notes in Your Book*

Don't forget to make notes in your book!

Tracing the Great Ideas*

Find quotes in these chapters that relate to the great ideas, or themes. Write down the quote with its page number on the corresponding Great Ideas Quotes pages provided (at the beginning of this guide). Keeping track of quotes will help you write the final theme essay(s)!

Example quotes and their themes

Great Ideas Quotes throughout the book for the theme *Myth, rhymes, legends as knowledge*

"A door. . . . I have heard of such things." (124)

Tell It Back*

Do an oral summary of your reading on a recording device or to another human being. Narrate the most important events in order while sharing the elements of the characters' development that are important.

Reading Questions

1. Why have the four children been sent to live with the old professor?

____

____

____

____

2. Mr. Tumnus tells Lucy that it's always winter in Narnia now, and never Christmas. What does this description tell readers about what it's like to live there?

____

____

____

____

____

____

*You'll see these icons at the beginning of each unit as a reminder to make notes, trace great ideas, and tell back what you've read.

3. Who does Edmund meet in Narnia? Give several details about their meeting.

Discussion Questions

1. Is Mr. Tumnus a morally good or bad character? Keep in mind Mr. Tumnus's planned cooperation with the White Witch. Explain your position.

2. Mr. Tumnus tells Lucy that it's always winter in Narnia now. What could the winter weather represent, and what are some of the ways that Lewis demonstrates its significance?

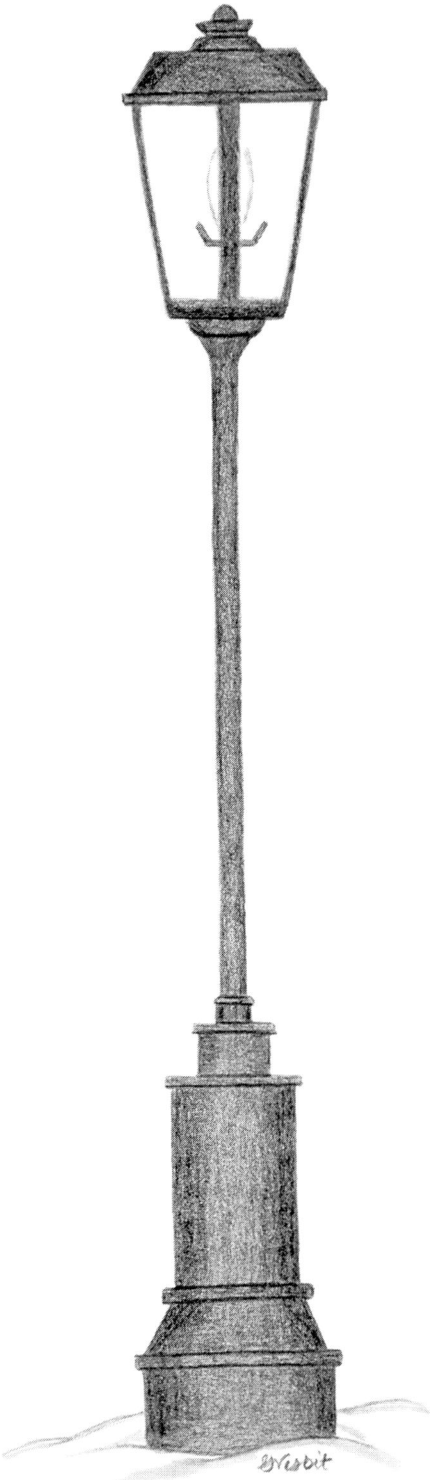

3. Compare Edmund and Lucy's personalities. What qualities from the essays do you begin to see taking root in these young lives? What is their personal responsibility for this, and what are external forces that shape their personalities?

Life Questions—Journaling Assignment

Feel free to respond to the life questions here or to keep them in a separate journal used for meditative contemplation.

1. Has there been a moment in your life (or that of a close friend or sibling, or perhaps a parent who has described a story from her youth) when, like Edmund, you were in very difficult circumstances and you felt the difficulty of making a good choice in the midst of them? Describe it.

2. Did you make a good choice or not? What happened? What were the consequences? What would you do now if faced with a similar situation?

Write Your Own Discussion Questions

1.

2.

Unit 2: Chapters 4–6

Make Notes in Your Book

Tracing the Great Ideas

Tell It Back

Reading Questions

1. How is the queen's Turkish delight enchanted?

2. What agreement does Edmund make with the queen and what motivates him to do it?

3. When Peter and Susan tell the professor Lucy's story, he says there are only three possibilities for Lucy's behavior. Explain the three possibilities.

Discussion Questions

1. The professor walks Peter and Susan through logical reasoning when they ask about Lucy. Can the professor's logical reasoning be applied to other educational situations or arguments?

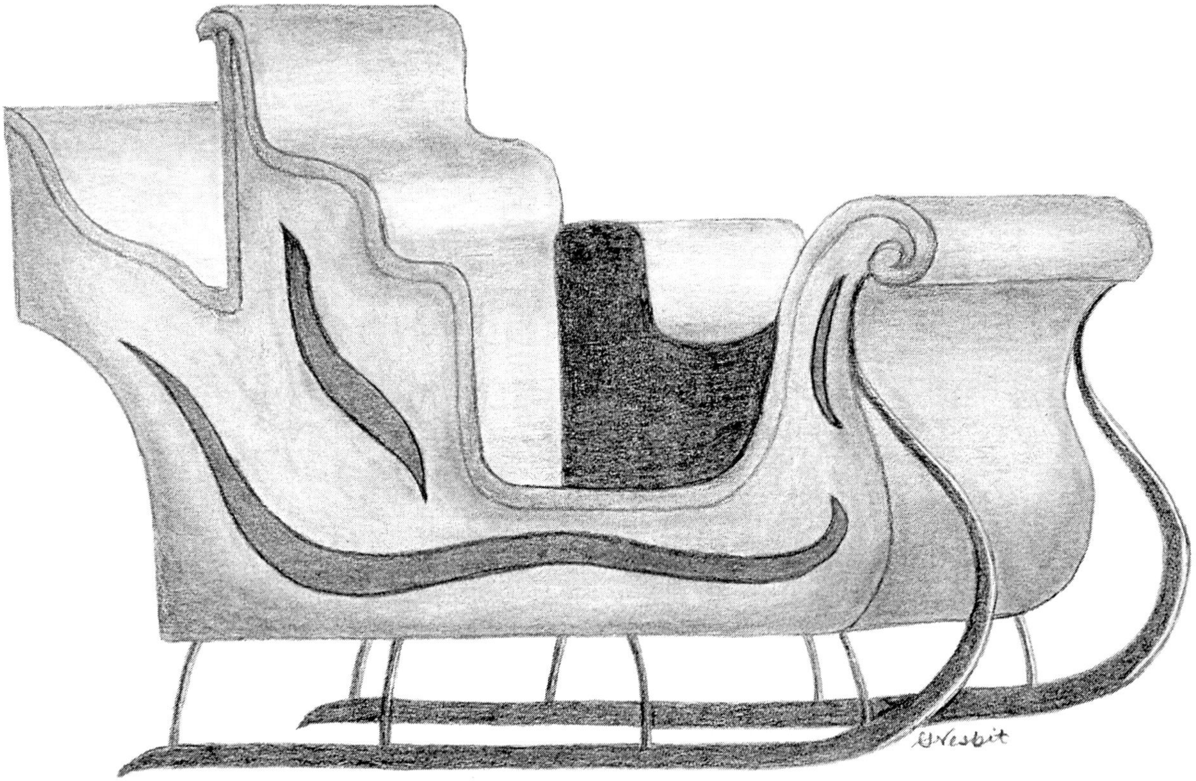

2. Unlike Lucy, Edmund has not heard the stories about the White Witch before he meets her. Could Edmund have realized in spite of his ignorance that the White Witch shouldn't be trusted and made a different choice?

3. Do the children have a responsibility to help Mr. Tumnus, or should they have returned to the spare room?

Life Questions—Journaling Assignment

Feel free to respond to the life questions here or to keep them in a separate journal used for meditative contemplation.

1. Reflect on the trilemma presented through Lucy's character and the professor's reflection—Christ was either telling the truth about Himself in the gospels (which is a strange truth indeed, like Lucy's), He was lying (and a scoundrel to deceive people on such a serious matter), or He was crazy (because you can't claim you are God and not be God and still be sane). What does this conclusion suggest about the claim that Christ was a good man, a moral model for us, or even a prophet?

2. Our own faith is conveyed to us in stories too. Are there aspects of the stories that make up our faith that are difficult for you to believe, or that create doubt in you? Does the fact that they are told as stories and not written like a science textbook help or hinder as you try to make sense of them? How does the choice of form (story versus textbook) instruct you as you work with these doubts and difficulties?

Write Your Own Discussion Questions

1.

2.

Unit 3: Chapters 7–9

Make Notes in Your Book

Tracing the Great Ideas

Tell It Back

Reading Questions

1. The beavers share two poems or rhymes with the children. How do these poems/rhymes communicate knowledge?

2. How does Edmund justify his decision to leave his siblings and motivate himself to continue traveling to the White Witch? You might want to consider the essay "The Great Sin."

3. Describe the White Witch's castle in detail. What information about the witch can you get from this setting?

Discussion Questions

1. What do the children feel at the mention of Aslan's name? Why might Edmund respond differently from his siblings?

2. Mr. Beaver shows the children Lucy's handkerchief to prove that they can trust him. Besides this token, what details does the author give about the beavers that let us know the beavers are virtuous?

3. When Edmund enters the queen's courtyard he finds stone statues. He uses a lead pencil to scribble on the stone statue. Why do you think Edmund feels compelled to make fun of the statue?

Life Questions—Journaling Assignment

Feel free to respond to the life questions here or to keep them in a separate journal used for meditative contemplation.

1. Describe a meal experience that was wonderful on account of the food, the company, and the atmosphere.

2. Reflect on a moment when you felt compelled to mock something sober because of your own misdeeds. If you can't think of such a moment, reflect on the things that inspire you to mockery or sarcasm. Why do you think they do this?

Write Your Own Discussion Questions

1.

2.

Unit 4: Chapters 10–12

Make Notes in Your Book

Tracing the Great Ideas

Tell It Back

Reading Questions

1. What is each child's gift from Father Christmas?

2. Why is the appearance of Father Christmas significant? How does his appearance relate to the changing landscape?

3. What happens when Susan blows her horn?

Discussion Questions

1. How does food represent the vice of the White Witch and the virtue of the beavers? Refer to chapters 4, 11, and 7.

2. In *The Screwtape Letters*, Lewis describes courage not as a virtue, but the form of all the virtues when tested. Do you agree with Lewis's statement? What virtues are tested during Peter's battle with the wolf?

3. The children meet Aslan for the first time in chapter 12. Aslan is described as both "good" and "terrible," which might be considered antonyms. How can both these attributes be true, or is it a contradiction?

Life Questions—Journaling Assignment

Feel free to respond to the life questions here or to keep them in a separate journal used for meditative contemplation.

1. What is a virtue that you possess? What were the influences that helped this to become a part of your character?

2. What is a virtue that you do not possess but desire to make a part of your life? Can you think of two or three things you could do to help yourself acquire this virtue?

Write Your Own Discussion Questions

1.

2.

Unit 5: Chapters 13–15

Make Notes in Your Book

Tracing the Great Ideas

Tell It Back

Reading Questions

1. Why does the queen come to Aslan's camp?

2. What instructions does Aslan give Peter? Why does he give him these instructions?

3. What happens when Lucy and Susan follow Aslan at night?

Discussion Questions

1. In chapter 13, Lewis (as the narrator) says that part of the queen's magic is making things look like something they are not. What is the relationship between deception and evil?

2. Why does Aslan have a better understanding of the deep magic than the White Witch?

3. After Aslan comes back to life, he begins running around and playing with Lucy and Susan (185). Aslan could have immediately gone to rescue the stone creatures and fight the White Witch, but he spends those moments playing. Why do you think Lewis decided to include this scene?

Life Questions—Journaling Assignment

Feel free to respond to the life questions here or to keep them in a separate journal used for meditative contemplation.

1. Can you think of a time in your own experience, or that of a close friend or family member, when evil looked beautiful or good or advantageous?

2. What moment in your life or what activity that you love reminds you of the joyous nature of the resurrection? Eric Liddell said, "When I run I feel God's pleasure." What is the eqivalent in your own experience?

____

____

____

____

____

____

____

Write Your Own Discussion Questions

1. ____

____

2. ____

____

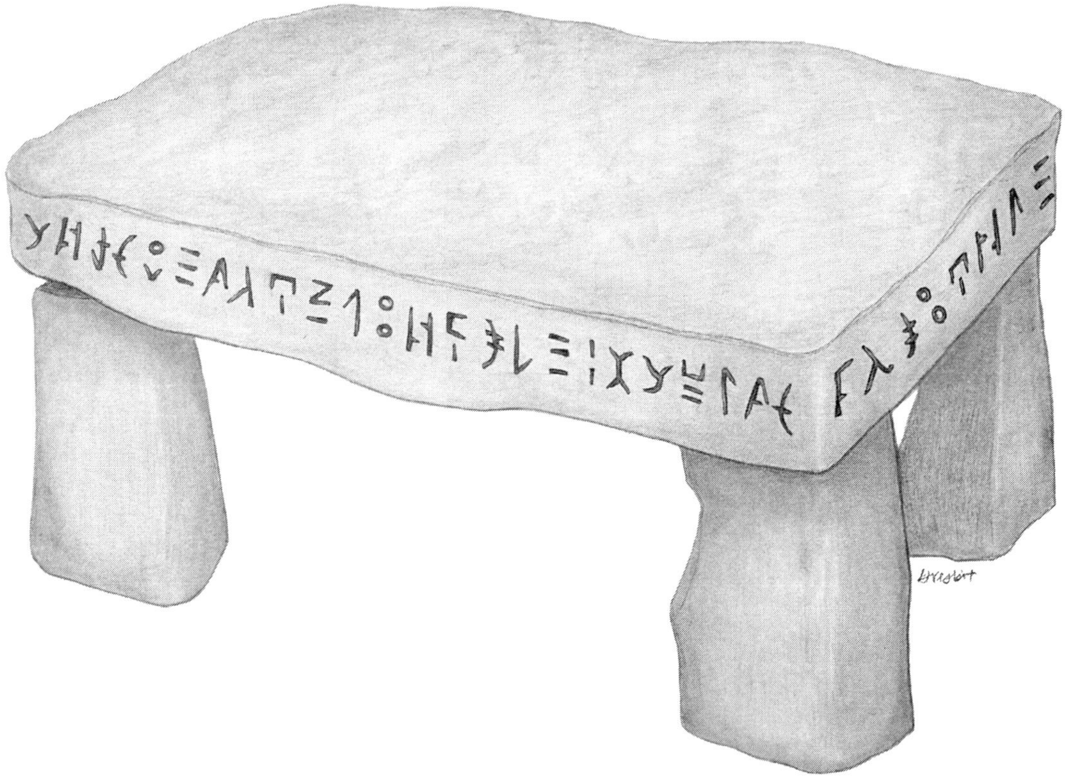

Unit 6: Chapters 16-17

Make Notes in Your Book

Tracing the Great Ideas

Tell It Back

Reading Questions

1. What is Lucy's job when she arrives on the battlefield?

2. What is the reign of Kings Peter and Edmund and Queens Susan and Lucy like? What are their royal epithets (a description that is attached at the end of someone's name)?

3. How do the four children leave Narnia?

Discussion Questions

1. Aslan breathes on the stone statues to turn them back into living creatures. Why do you think Lewis uses this method to revive creatures?

2. What images, colors, and sounds does Lewis use to describe the transformation of the White Witch's castle? Why would Lewis include this description?

3. When the children return from Narnia, no time has passed. What do you think is the significance of Narnia existing outside of Earth's time stream?

Life Questions—Journaling Assignment

Feel free to respond to the life questions here or to keep them in a separate journal used for meditative contemplation.

1. Remember Meilaender's essay "Theology in Stories," which gave us the metaphor for God as author of the book of our lives? How does it impact you as you read this story (*The Lion, the Witch and the Wardrobe*) about another world? Does it make that possibility more real in your own life? What does Narnia's world add to your imagination?

2. Have you ever experienced the world as colorful and vibrant as it was when the statues came to life in Narnia? Does this scene feel real to you, even though you haven't been inside of it exactly?

Write Your Own Discussion Questions

1.

2.

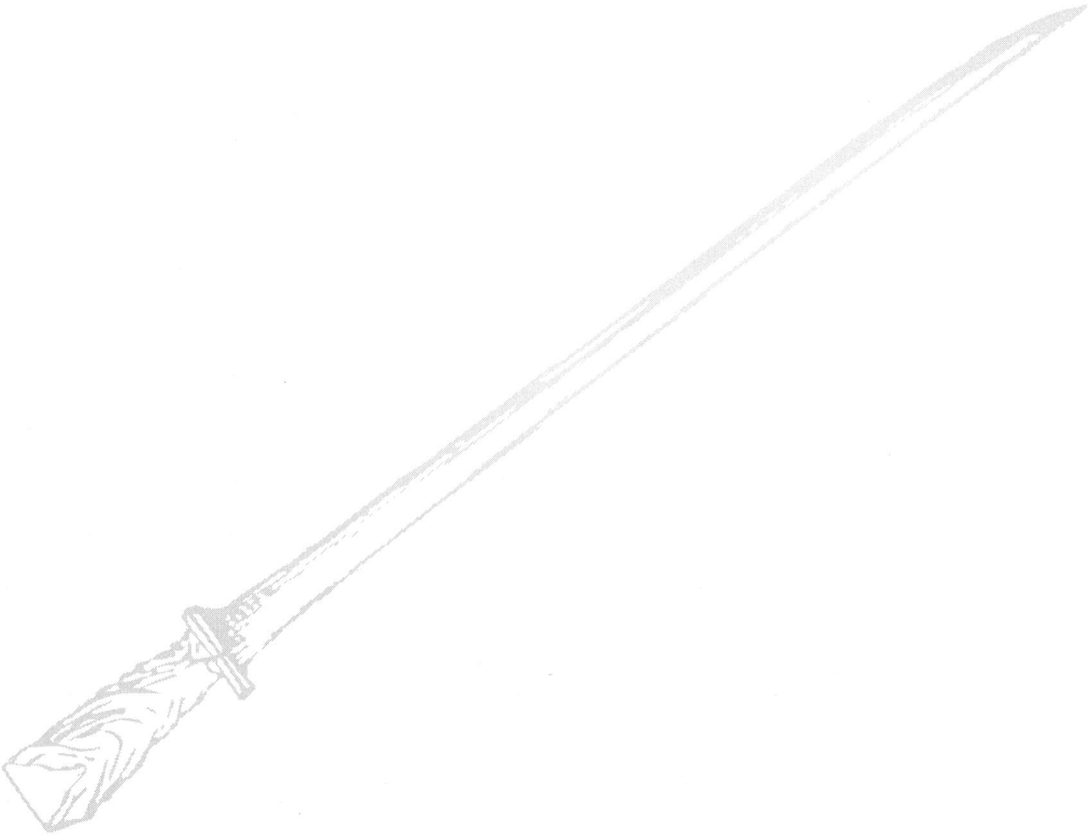

Quotation Identification

We have chosen memorable quotations from each unit that are significant to *The Lion, The Witch and the Wardrobe* and that guide you through the great ideas you have studied. Identify who said each quote and give a sentence or two that describes the context of the quote within the moment of the story.

Unit 1 (Chapter 2)

They had titles like *The Life and Letters of Silenus* or *Nymphs and Their Ways* or *Men, Monks and Gamekeepers: A Study in Popular Legend* or *Is Man a Myth?*

Unit 2 (Chapter 5)

"Logic! . . . Why don't they teach logic at these schools? There are only three possibilities. Either your sister is telling lies, or she is mad, or she is telling the truth."

Unit 3 (Chapter 8)

"Turn *him* into stone? If she can stand on her two feet and look him in the face it'll be the most she can do and more than I expect of her."

Unit 4 (Chapter 11)

And __________, for the first time in this story, felt sorry for someone besides himself.

Unit 5 (Chapter 15)

"Aren't you dead then, dear Aslan?"

Unit 6 (Chapter 16)

Instead of all that deadly white the courtyard was now a blaze of colours; glossy chestnut sides of centaurs, indigo horns of unicorns, dazzling plumage of birds. . . . And instead of the deadly silence the whole place rang with the sound of happy roarings, brayings, yelpings, barkings, squealings, cooings . . .

Enrichment Activities

1. Watch the movie *The Lion, the Witch and the Wardrobe* with a group of friends. Do a comparison of the book and the movie after you watch it together (we recommend taking some notes). Be sure to learn a bit about "reading" films. In addition to talking about how the director did or did not capture the characters, the plot sequence, and the special wonder of the book which is made up of several difficult-to-name factors, such as the atmosphere of the book, talk about how he failed or succeeded in filmmaking—lighting, types of shots, text included or cut out, landscape, costume, etc.

   Please note: Your Great Ideas essay could also be on the movie-book comparison. Don't forget to use specific references from both the written text and the film text. Be specific.

   (Optional) Make a meal or snacks for the movie based on food enjoyed in Narnia: Turkish delight (buy it from a local candy store), creamy potatoes, grilled fish, tea and toast with jam, etc.

2. Draw a picture or make a graphic picture of a scene in this book. Render it according to the way the story makes you feel. Or make a digital book cover according to what you think should be emphasized in relation to the book. What "argument" are you making about the book based on the image that you create?

3. Choose a sizable passage (or several) from *The Lion, the Witch and the Wardrobe* to memorize and recite to your class or family. Choose something that is particularly important to what you need to learn, focus on, internalize—something that will challenge you or remind you in the ways that you need to be challenged. Work on elocution: your posture, diction, facial expression, and verbal expression. Attempt to use all of the same emphases and intonations that your character might have used.

Alternative Writing Projects

Instead of an expository essay as described in the next section, your teacher may consider the following writing assignments that also help you reflect on the great ideas of *The Lion, the Witch and the Wardrobe*:

1. **Create a conversation** between two or three of the characters in Narnia on one of the themes for which you took notes. Make it true to their character, language, and the kinds of observations these characters would make.
2. **Write a letter** to a friend or relative in which you try to explain what you are learning about the theme you choose from *The Lion, the Witch and the Wardrobe*. Be sure to include characters, plot, and images, not just ideas and information. Consider it in light of a problem with which you have been struggling that you feel the story "answers."
3. **Research project 1:** Do some research on what was happening in history at the time that Lewis was writing and publishing the books (approximately 1948–1954, but start with the World War II era). Find references in the book that allude to the historical context. Write about Lewis's attitude toward that period of history in light of the book's portrayals (i.e., secret police, totalitarian rule, etc.).
4. **Research project 2:** Do some research on the references that Lewis makes in the *The Lion, the Witch and the Wardrobe* to stories outside the story he is writing—these include myths, fairy tales, and legends that have a life of their own outside of his story. You can also include stories or characters that people think might be sources for Lewis's book. Some examples: Father Time, the White Witch (Lilith, Circe, and witches in fairy tales).

Great Ideas Essay Assignments

As you write the expository essay described below, remember that Lewis said that how you feel about a story is teaching you about the story as much as anything else. For instance, a student once wrote in response to this book: "The first and second time I read this book, the end was heartbreaking to me. It seemed like a magnificent dream was ending or a perfect feeling was being replaced by [a return to] normalcy. I have not figured out why (though I have thought about it for many minutes) and it still bothers me." The book, in this student's case, stirred *Sehnsucht*—Lewis's idea of inconsolable longing—and that is part of its meaning. In many ways it is the embodiment of "The Weight of Glory"—that sense we all have that we were meant for a place such as Narnia and adventures such as we had in Narnia, that there must be a door that leads us out into a world that contains the depth of experience that we perceive we should be having in this transcendent life.

The Great Ideas essays require you to present Lewis's view on the themes we introduced at the beginning of this guide and traced through our reading. Choose one of the great ideas that you followed throughout the book. Develop a thesis in which you are saying something specific, making a claim about this theme. If you would like to use our description of the great idea as your thesis and write a paper defending it, you are welcome to do that. If you are interested in coming up with your own thesis, we invite you to do so. You will be defending your thesis in a logical essay format, using your own language, metaphors, and illustrations. Notice how having kept notes and traced Great Ideas Quotes for these themes all through your reading, in addition to discussion, prepares you to expand on one of the themes for your essay. Use characters, plot, and imagery to develop your essay.

Our main goal here is to help you begin making connections and forming arguments about ideas that run throughout a book. You have sorted the pieces of the puzzle into piles of similar colors (by reading, marking the book, taking notes, answering questions, and having discussions); now you can put the puzzle together (the difference being a puzzle has one way to go together, but themes can be discussed and argued in endless ways). When building your thesis, choose a question that has particular significance in your own life—perhaps one that you have struggled with or has been particularly challenging in your own life or the life of your family. This will make your writing stronger and more purposeful. Keep in mind that there are countless ways to complete this assignment. The following elements will help to guide you regardless of the thesis that you choose.

Tips for Writing a Great Essay

- Support your thesis with the essays you read alongside this book.
- Develop your ideas with examples.
- Help us to see with description how your examples prove your argument.
- Explain your quotations and how they fit your argument.
- Consider what argument someone might make against yours and address those concerns as part of your defense.
- Conclude by restating your thesis with the depth of understanding you have established in the course of the writing.

For each great idea we have given the topic and thesis and posed the question the thesis is addressing. In terms of the length of your essay, your teacher may want you to write as little as 250 words (approximately 1 page) or may desire a more developed essay along the lines of 1,250 words (approximately 5 pages). See the teacher's edition for sample essays.

Great Ideas Essay on *Myth, Rhymes, Legends as Knowledge*

Thesis:

The Lion, the Witch and the Wardrobe can be classified as children's literature or fantasy, and also bears striking characteristics of a myth or a legend. Not only does the whole novel feel like a myth, but myths, legends, prophecies, and rhymes play a significant role in the story.

Question:

What is the purpose of myth, rhyme, and legend in *The Lion, the Witch and the Wardrobe*?

Expanded Question:

What is the purpose of myth, rhyme, and legend in *The Lion, the Witch and the Wardrobe*? How does an appreciation of myth, legend, and rhyme enrich our lives? Using your knowledge of Lewis's personal life, describe how understanding myth influenced his faith.

Personal Connection:

Can you think of an instance in your own experience where myth, stories, rhymes, and legends were useful to you? This will help you to consider the theme. Be sure to clarify with your teacher whether or not the essay should include personal content and from what point of view it should be written.

Notes:

Great Ideas Essay on *Virtue and Moral Choice*

Thesis:

The plot of *The Lion, the Witch and the Wardrobe* moves forward because characters make moral choices, to do the virtuous thing or the wrong thing, and then everyone has to bear the consequences. Some virtues in *The Lion, the Witch and the Wardrobe* are charity (Christian love), forgiveness, courage, and selflessness.

Question:

What choices are considered virtuous in *The Lion, the Witch and the Wardrobe*?

Expanded Question:

How does Lewis show characters' virtues (or lack of) through their choices? Consider charity and forgiveness in particular. Describe also how one instance of virtue leads to the next in a particular situation in this story.

Personal Connection:

Has someone acting out of virtue ever affected you? Were you ever able to continue doing the right thing because you took that first step in the right direction? Be sure to clarify with your teacher whether or not the essay should include personal content and from what point of view it should be written.

Notes:

Great Ideas Essay on *Education/The Testing or Ordeal*

Thesis:

Childhood is often equated with education. We expect children to constantly learn new things and add to their collection of knowledge. The Pevensie siblings enter Narnia as children, still in that age of learning.

Question:

How do the Pevensie children learn about themselves?

Expanded Question:

What is the importance of the ordeal (or test)? Which characters face tests, and how could these tests be considered education? What are other characteristics of a good education?

Personal Connection:

What experiences or tests have you gone through that shaped how you view yourself? Be sure to clarify with your teacher whether or not the essay should include personal content and from what point of view it should be written.

Notes:

Great Ideas Essay on *Evil and Vice*

Thesis:

When the Pevensie children arrive in Narnia, they find a land suffering under the weight of an evil ruler. They soon discover that they are in the center of the struggle against evil and good, between the witch and Aslan.

Question:

How do evil and vice work? Consider the characters Edmund and the White Witch.

Expanded Question:

What is the nature of evil and what is its relationship to goodness? How do the characters Edmund and the White Witch illustrate the characteristics of evil and vice?

Personal Connection:

Evil is often deceptive. Have you or anyone you know gone down the wrong road because you believed a lie? Be sure to clarify with your teacher whether or not the essay should include personal content and from what point of view it should be written.

Notes:

Great Ideas Essay on *Landscape*

Thesis:

The landscape of Narnia goes through a radical change in *The Lion, the Witch and the Wardrobe.* When Lucy first enters, Narnia is held under the cold spell of winter. However, as Aslan arrives, so does spring.

Question:

How does the landscape symbolize the spiritual condition of Narnia?

Expanded Question:

What do you notice about the land and its value and significance to the story? Why do you think as readers we are not surprised that the witch is associated with winter and Aslan with spring?

Personal Connection:

How does the motif of the land affect you as a reader? What time of year do you respond to and why? Be sure to clarify with your teacher whether or not the essay should include personal content and from what point of view it should be written.

Notes:

Great Ideas Essay on *Responding to Aslan*/Sehnsucht

Thesis:

The way that characters respond to Aslan seems to be of utmost significance in this and all the Narnian Chronicles. Even Aslan's name evokes a response.

Question:

How do different characters respond to Aslan?

Expanded Question:

How do different characters respond to Aslan? How does this response signify their spiritual state?

Personal Connection:

Have you ever responded to anything the way the children do when they first hear Aslan's name? Which character do you identify with? Be sure to clarify with your teacher whether or not the essay should include personal content and from what point of view it should be written.

Notes:

Great Ideas Essay on *Multiple Worlds*

Thesis:

The Lion, the Witch and the Wardrobe spans two worlds—ours and Narnia. The children are sent to the professor's house during the London bombing raids of World War II, while Narnia is under the oppressive rule of the White Witch.

Question:

What is the relationship between Narnia and our world? How are they connected?

Expanded Question:

What is the relationship between these two worlds? How does the narrator help us bridge these worlds? What are some images or symbols in Narnia that parallel things in our world? Look also for the references to history—such as the totalitarian state, the secret police, or the bombings in London.

Personal Connection:

Have you ever considered the possibility of alternative worlds? What does the possibility of different worlds open up in our thinking about heaven and earth or time and eternity? Be sure to clarify with your teacher whether or not the essay should include personal content and from what point of view it should be written.

Notes:

Great Ideas Essay on *Deep Magic*

Thesis:

The White Witch approaches Aslan at his camp and demands Edmund's life on the basis of deep magic. In Narnia, deep magic is law; it determines how things work and is recognized by both Aslan and the White Witch as an authority. However, Aslan and the White Witch have a different level of understanding of the deep magic.

Question:

What is the deep magic and how does it work?

Expanded Question:

What is the deep magic and deeper magic, and how do they work? Compare Aslan's understanding with the witch's understanding of deep magic. Why does the witch not understand the deep magic as well as Aslan?

Personal Connection:

Does Narnia's deep magic remind you of anything in this world? Be sure to clarify with your teacher whether or not the essay should include personal content and from what point of view it should be written.

Notes:

Great Ideas Essay on *Forgiveness*

Thesis:

In his nonfiction writing, Lewis discusses the importance of forgiveness—a forgiveness that is quite different from an excuse. This forgiveness is costly. In Narnia, Lewis dramatically illustrates forgiveness of Edmund.

Question:

According to his essay "On Forgiveness," what is C.S. Lewis's definition of forgiveness? How is this illustrated in *The Lion, the Witch and the Wardrobe*?

Expanded Question:

According to his essay "On Forgiveness," what is C.S. Lewis's definition of forgiveness? How is this illustrated in *The Lion, the Witch and the Wardrobe*? What's the result of this forgiveness?

Personal Connection:

How does Lewis's concept of forgiveness challenge your own assumptions or practices of forgiveness? Be sure to clarify with your teacher whether or not the essay should include personal content and from what point of view it should be written.

Notes:

Appendix A: Lewis and Tolkien's View on Myth, and Myth Become Fact

At one point in his life, early in his relationship with Tolkien, Lewis saw myths as "lies and therefore worthless, even though breathed through silver,"[1] but Tolkien defended them as vehicles for truth. (He even wrote a poem for Lewis on the subject called "Mythopoeia.") Tolkien's answer was that they are not lies. At that moment in the conversation there was, Lewis wrote, "a rush of wind which came so suddenly on the still, warm evening and sent so many leaves pattering down that we thought it was raining. We held our breath."[2] Tolkien said about this scene:

> You look at trees . . . and call them "trees," and probably you do not think twice about the word. You call a star a "star," and think nothing more of it. But you must remember that these words, "tree," "star," were (in their original forms) names given to these objects by people with very different views from yours. To you, a tree is simply a vegetable organism, and a star simply a ball of inanimate matter moving along a mathematical course. But the first men to talk of "trees" and "stars" saw things very differently. To them, the world was alive with mythological beings. They saw the stars as living silver bursting into flame in answer to the eternal music. They saw the sky as a jeweled tent, and the earth as the womb whence all living things have come. To them, the whole of creation was "myth-woven and elf-patterned."[3]

Tolkien argued that knowledge and seeing means moving beyond knowing what stars are made of (flaming gas), and because of our fallenness and finitude we can only do this through the imagination with image, metaphor, and myth. Lewis's response to this statement was to wonder whether or not we create Christianity because we want to believe in something like it. This is how Freud viewed religious conviction—something we make up because we desire it to be true; he called it "wish fulfillment." Tolkien responded by asking, "Whence came the wish and whence the power to dream?" In other words, if materialist philosophy about myth is true, why do we even have these desires and wishes? What (or Who) gave us this longing and the joy itself? Tolkien forced Lewis to consider that, as Alan Jacobs puts it, "It was not Joy itself but its presence in a biological organism comprising largely water, nitrogen and carbon that constituted the greatest puzzle. That we dream and wish *at all* is a powerful element of the case for belief that myths communicate some truth that cannot be communicated any other way."[4]

The craving for myths suggests the presence of a need they satisfy or try to satisfy. They reach something deep within us; because they do not and cannot meet the need they invoke, our experience with them is characterized by longing. The Christian myth is distinguished from the other myths in the sense that it is the true fulfillment of them—the enactment of their foretelling. It was an historical event versus an imagined story. Lewis wrote this about his evening spent with Tolkien and Dyson on Addison's Walk:

> Now what Dyson and Tolkien showed me was this: that if I met the idea of sacrifice in a Pagan story I didn't mind it at all: and again, that if I met the idea of god sacrificing himself to himself . . . I liked it very much and was mysteriously moved by it; again, that the idea of the dying and reviving God (Balder, Adonis, Bacchus) similarly moved me provided I met it anywhere *except* in the Gospels. The reason was that in Pagan stories I was prepared to feel the myth as profound and suggestive of meanings beyond my grasp even tho' I could not say in cold prose "what it meant."

1. Humphrey Carpenter, *The Inklings* (New York: Ballentine Books, 1978), 46.
2. Carpenter, 46.
3. Carpenter, 46.
4. Alan Jacobs, *The Narnian: The Life and Imagination of C.S. Lewis* (New York: HarperSanFrancisco, 2005), 145–146. For an excellent summary of this book, download the Mars Hill interview of Jacobs with Ken Myers at https://marshillaudio.org/catalog/alan-jacobs-narnian.

> **Now the story of Christ is simply a true myth: a myth working on us in the same way as the others, but with the tremendous difference that it *really happened*:** and one must be content to accept it in the same way, remembering that it is God's myth where the others are men's myths: i.e. the Pagan stories are God expressing himself through the minds of poets, using such images as He found there, while Christianity is God expressing himself through "real things" [bold added].[5]

Lewis believed that all the stories that spoke of dying gods were anticipating (without knowing it) the fact of the dying God in the person of Christ. He believed that deeply lodged within us is an unconscious knowledge of such a Savior and that knowledge spanned centuries anticipating the factual arrival in time and space of Christ. Likewise, he believed that the Christian story partakes of the tradition of myth and storytelling and uses the power of that genre in seeking to speak powerfully to the human psyche to reveal God to the world.

> Now as myth transcends thought, Incarnation transcends myth. The heart of Christianity is a myth which is also fact. The old myth of the Dying God, *without ceasing to be myth*, comes down from the heaven of legend and imagination to the earth of history. It *happens*—at a particular date, in a particular place, followed by definable historical consequences.[6]

5. Jacobs, *Narnian*, 148–149.

6. C.S. Lewis, "Myth Became Fact" in *God in the Dock* (Grand Rapids: Eerdmans, 1970), 66.

"On Forgiveness"

Reading Questions

1. Why does Lewis say many people, especially in wartime, don't like forgiveness?

2. Who is the one person we show the right type of forgiveness toward?

3. Lewis says reading a story in a newspaper that is false can be a litmus test (a way to prove or disprove) of hating the sin instead of the sinner. How does this test work?

Discussion Questions

1. Is it beneficial to love others exactly how we love ourselves?

2. Can a Christian be a soldier?

3. On the surface, Christian morality seems similar to secular, humanistic morality. For example, secular governments outlaw murder and theft. Most people consider kindness and courage virtues. Both Christians and non-Christians convict people of crimes and enforce penalties, sometimes even death sentences. Is there a difference between a Christian and secular morality?

"The Great Sin" and "Charity"

Reading Questions

1. What is the great sin?

2. What is the essential nature of pride? Explain

3. What is Lewis's definition of charity?

Discussion Questions

1. Is pride the greatest sin? Why or why not?

2. Can pride ever be considered a good thing?

3. Should people feel charitable when they help others? Does the action matter more than the attitude, or do insincere motives undermine their charity?

"The Weight of Glory"

Reading Questions

1. According to Lewis, what do non-Christians believe the highest virtue is? How is this "virtue" described?

2. What are the five main points that Lewis lists about heaven?

3. According to Lewis, what do people want with beauty, besides seeing it?

Discussion Questions

1. Should Christians seek a reward?

2. What is Lewis's concept of glory?

3. Can poetry—imaginary images and ideas—be true?

"Theology in Stories" by Gilbert Meilaender

Reading Questions

1. In *The Voyage of the Dawn Treader*, what spell does Lucy find while reading? What happens when she tries to find the spell again?

2. What does *Sehnsucht* mean?

3. Which ancient theologian does Meilaender say comes closest to explaining the combination of God's grace and free will in his writings? What is the title and genre of his book?

Discussion Questions

1. According to Meilaender, is life similar to stories?

2. Meilaender uses the critic Stephen Crites to explain some of C.S. Lewis's ideas. Crites discusses how people try to resolve the tension between the longing for eternal universals and the earthly particulars. There are two different paths to escape this tension, which correspond to the "North" and "South" in Lewis's book *Pilgrim's Regress*. What are these two escapes? Are they problematic?

"Sometimes Fairy Stories May Say Best What's to Be Said" by C.S. Lewis

Reading Questions

1. According to Lewis, what are the two components necessary for something to be worth writing? Explain them.

2. What are characteristics of a fairy tale?

3. How did Lewis first start writing *The Lion, the Witch and the Wardrobe*? What was his author's motive?

4. What was Lewis's motive as a man to write *The Lion, the Witch and the Wardrobe*?

Notes

Notes

Notes

Notes

the art of
POETRY

If you have ever felt mystified by, or unable to enjoy the significance of poetry, this book will lead you step-by-step to understanding and love of this branch of literature, guided by a gifted poet and teacher. *The Art of Poetry* is an excellent middle school or high school curriculum; it teaches the practice of reading a poem slowly and carefully and introduces students to the elements of poetry (such as imagery and metaphor) and the many forms that can make a poem, from sonnet to open verse. In the belief that practice is the best way to learn, this book is rich with explications, exercises, and activities. A biography of each poet is also included, along with a CD of a reading of many of the poems.

From the Introduction:

There has never been a civilization without poetry. From the beginning of time, people have sought to turn their thoughts, feelings, and stories into memorable speech to share with others. Using language, the poet preserves something precious in the world by allowing us to live next to her, to see what she sees, to enter the experience she has built for us with her words and attention to the moment. Poetry acknowledges something deep within our nature—an urge to name, say, sing, grieve, praise, out of our solitariness, to another person. It makes words into a material thing, hard and solid as a table, dense with significance.

Find samples and more information at www.ClassicalAcademicPress.com.

Want to know more about the author? Check out her poetry blog at:
www.ArtOfPoetryOnline.com.

“In her clear-eyed, passionate, and accessible account of the power poetry plays in our lives and in her careful and exact explanation of its craft, Christine Perrin provides an inspiring, accessible, and comprehensive introduction to the reading and writing of poetry. What I admire most about *The Art of Poetry* is how it proceeds from Perrin's deeply lived and felt convictions about the necessity of poetry and from her experience as a gifted poet.”

—Michael Collier, Former Poet Laureate of Maryland; Professor of Creative Writing, University of Maryland; Director of the Bread Loaf Writer's Conference

Walking to Wisdom Literature Guides:
The Inklings Collection

Stories give us an experience of certain knowledge, which is why how we feel about the book is part of what the book is teaching us. We have kept this idea in heart and mind while making the Walking to Wisdom Literature Guides: The Inklings Collection to be used in conjunction with the works of C.S. Lewis, J.R.R. Tolkien, and Dorothy Sayers. We have named them "Walking to Wisdom Literature Guides" because acquiring wisdom often happens at the pace of a walk and benefits from having a mentor. We have sought to guide students through these marvelous books as well as imparting to them the skill of reading.

CLASSICAL ACADEMIC PRESS
Classical Subjects Creatively Taught